B.R.E.A.T.H.E. AGAIN

VISIONARY

Dr. Obioma Martin

8 Women Share their Stories of Restoration, Faith & Hope

Copyright © 2020 by Dr. Obioma Martin

ISBN# 978-1-7360578-0-3

All rights reserved. No parts of this publication may be reproduced, distributed, or transmitted in any form or by any means, including photocopying, recording, or other electronic or mechanical methods without the prior written permission of the visionary. For permission request, solicit the visionary
Dr. Obioma Martin

@ obioma@obiomamartin.com

Publishing Company

OmazingYou

Wynnewood, Pa 19096

Contents

About the Visionary 1

Introduction 3

DEDICATION 4

Wanda Lovale McCall: Letting Go What You Know 5

Anesha Bonelli: Believe the Process of Forgiveness 15

Camellia Burkett-Graham: Release the Bondage. 25

Shanita Vital Davis: Embrace change. 31

Dr. Victoria Sherlock: Accept What God Allows Your story does not belong to you 37

La Vonne A. Weaver: Take Action Turning Challenges Into Works of Art 43

Mavis A. Creagh: Heal from Self Pain 53

Pastor Cynthia D. Allen: Elevation requires Alleviation. 61

About the Visionary

Obioma Martin is an international transformational speaker, B.R.E.A.T.H.E. accountability-coach, Amazon bestselling author, small business expert, childcare strategist, and esteemed advocate for women's empowerment. Martin's passion for equipping women with the tools they need to not only survive but prosper and live audaciously has launched her into a life of unparalleled servitude, wherein she continues to thrive by helping others.

Martin has helped over 5000 women get off welfare and get the credentials required to complete and further their education. A life-long learner herself, Martin holds multiple degrees; associates in Early Childhood Education, Bachelor's in Childcare Management, a master's degree in Early Childhood Education and Leadership, an Honorary Doctorate from MizCEO Society for Coaches, Goldman Sachs 10,000 Small Business Program alumni, certified biblical counselor, and an ordained evangelist.

Contact Martin at obioma@obiomamartin.com

Follow her on FB@obiomamartin.com, IG@iamobiomamartin.com

Website www.omazingyou.com

Introduction

Breathe Again is a collection of stories from courageous women who have overcome hardships, trials, disappointments, and heartbreak. I am confident that you will see yourself in one of these stories. These stories are empowering and uplifting. At the end of each story, the author shares how they overcame their situations through faith. They believed in God, released negative people, places, and things, embraced change, accepted what God allowed, took action, healed, and then elevated.

DEDICATION

This book is dedicated to women everywhere, young and mature. It is my desire to help women get unstuck in every area of their lives and remove the barriers that prevent them from breathing and enjoying life.

To my one and only daughter, Jael Maxwell, my mother, Gloria A. Brown, my sisters, every student, mentee, and client, this book is for you. I listened to your stories, your struggles, and your journey. This book is for you.

Wanda Lovale McCall
Letting Go What You Know

You are far too creative to be limited by fear, finances, familial limitations, and well-meaning friends. It's time to let go of what you know. In 1500 words or less, I am about to help you release one of the most important things you own.

The Vision.

The Vision is different from "a vision." A simple vision is the expectation of a desired outcome that makes us happy on an emotional or personal level. It involves the creative energy of imagination and the ability to see or think about something that is to come. In contrast, The Vision is divine, disruptive, and destiny altering. It is the place where purpose, gifting, and anointing meet.

There are tons of teachings on purpose and anointing, but I would like to share with you the power of releasing your gifts within this chapter. When we release our gifts, we activate the anointing and come into alignment so that purpose is fulfilled. Our gifts can bring spiritual endowments from God or natural abilities that flow in our life with ease or have been obtained through focus and experience.

Letting Go What You Know

When we speak of letting go from a personal growth perspective, we often focus on releasing pain from the past, self-limiting thoughts, or toxic relationships. All of this is super important for personal freedom and opening our hearts to divine flow. However, I want to discuss a different type of letting go, letting go what you know.

This type of release is the process by which we speak to teach and empower others with our story and our experiences. This is when we open our mouth to connect and create with our words the outcomes needed and desired. It is the second step of biblical manifestation and often requires confidence to perform.

> **"Joseph had a dream, and when he told it to his brothers, they hated him all the more" Genesis 37:5**

Letting go of what you know will require your tongue, your mouth, and His words. This super combo of natural and spiritual movement will release the God-breathed vision in your heart into the Earth. Will this require boldness? Sure will. Will I be misunderstood, laughed at, celebrated, or supported? Perhaps all those things will happen. For sure, all things are the recipe for success.

The bible gives the account of Joseph, the favorite son of Jacob, who had a particular gift. He was a dreamer. His dreams were prophetic in nature, meaning they foretold of things to come in the future. In addition, Joseph had the anointing of a strategist, which led to economic gain for those he served. In the book of Genesis, we read his story in chapters 37, 39-47. The theme of his life is blessing, and it is affirmed by his name Joseph which means "increase." Joseph found himself in one situation after another, yet he would rise to the occasion because he released his gift. If you have not read his entire story, take some time in the next few days and read it.

It is important to realize that his story is in Genesis, which means "firsts." The book of Genesis is a book of precedents. That means as dynamic women of faith, we can look to this book as a guide on how the Kingdom of God operates. We know it operates first by seeing, then speaking, and next doing.

Seeing, Speaking, Doing

If you are anything like me, the quiet, creative, visionary type, you have no problem seeing. And I mean seeing all sorts of things. We almost get blindsided by one new project after another, not capable of fully completing that last one we started. Speaking is a little different. Sure we can tell the vision to a few people here and there but getting bold, vocal, and visible with it is a challenge. It's a challenge because we are afraid of a potentially negative response or no response at all. Still, we must move forward and release the vision with our mouths and His words NOW.

In Joseph's story, his first vision from God regarding his rise to power was not received well. He had another dream and spoke it again regardless. In so doing, he set the vision in motion. This is what you need to do, my friend. Speak the vision and set things in motion.

The vision will always include the use of your gift. With this in mind, you need to look for every opportunity to serve with your gifting. Well, how do I do that, you may ask? It is simple… By talking about what you do. Catch your community's attention and release the talent and treasure Heaven has placed in you. We know by precedent that God loves to make a scene and show up in wildly amazing ways with His people so let's give Him the opportunity.

Once all eyes are on, seize the opening you need to do the work you love in the industry that needs your gift the most. Take those speaking invites, look for opportunities to collaborate with others, bless individuals with your knowledge, and keep momentum. The more you do this, the more doors will manifest for you to walk through. God will have your name spoken in rooms where you are not. People will seek you out; just you wait and see!

Get Vocal and Visible with Vision

At the time of this writing, I recently finished hosting a challenge group for a faith community on sharing their testimony. It's the 5-Day Push Challenge, and men and women left this challenge empowered to not only share their testimonies but also share their talents. We were blown away at just how gifted people in our community are right now. And we would not have known until they released what they knew through what they do.

Here are some tips in this season to let go of what you know:

- *Create a blog*
- This can be as simple as creating a Facebook business page and writing posts daily to teach, inform, or inspire others.

Start a small group

This can be done virtually and or in-person. You can build others with like-minded interests so that they achieve goals or make an impact in areas vital to them.

Teach a course

With so many platforms available to you, there is no excuse why you can not teach other women new skills. Utilize webinar platforms, live-streaming apps, or community spaces as available to educate from your knowledge.

Go Live!

That's right! Open your mouth wide, and the Lord will fill it, Sis! Talk about your life, experiences, and challenges. Pray for others, live. Share your passion projects live, declare what God is saying in dark, challenging times, whatever it is

JUST GO!

Use social media as a tool. It is giving so much leverage to everyday people like you and I. We would not waste this powerful advantage to get seen and heard for free. You can do this. Getting vocal and visible is not easy, but once you start and stay consistent, momentum picks up, and the benefits of letting go of what you know will quickly surpass the challenge you feel.

Here is a declaration for you to speak daily

Release

Today I share my gifts with women Holy Spirit is bringing into my path

I create connections with women who desire the service I provide with my gift.

I pour out, and I am filled. I pour out, and I am filled.

I have moved from fear to faith, and I increase in confidence as I share your purpose that is at work in and through me. I see my significance in the world. I speak and get results.

The vision and gift in and on me attract the talent and the resources to help me grow and flow for the profit of the kingdom, the community, my family, and me. As I grow, Heaven is increasing my support.

I am not overwhelmed.

I am overjoyed.

I Release

Heaven is Waiting for You

There is no change in the Earth without a challenge. Getting vocal and visible is such a challenge. However, Heaven needs your words and your work to assist you with the vision. Each time you open your mouth, you empower your soul to do the work. Each time you speak the Word of God, angels are empowered to provide divine support.

As you release, important things shift and happen:

- Creativity increases
- Lives are transformed
- Mentors come into your life
- God raises up supporters
- Financial flow moves toward the vision
- Confidence builds as growth in your gift expands
- So RELEASE!

It's time to let go what you know.

Wanda Lovale McCall is a faith focused, engaging speaker and leading expert at helping women reframe fear of judgment so they become confident communicators.

Wanda is the author of the book Ok, Judge Me, creator of the Girl on Fire training series and is a dynamic biblical teacher and women's inspirational speaker. She has been a keynote speaker, workshop presenter and panelist for various women's conferences. With over 18 years of nursing and ministry service she seeks to educate women on how to challenge the fear in their head so they live and lead from fire in their heart. While Wanda loves speaking and inspiring women, she loves her husband Nate, two daughters Namarah and Seanna more. They live right outside the city of cheesesteaks and soft pretzels in Cherry Hill, New Jersey.

She is the founder of Live Inside Out, LLC. She is the creator of My Powerplace™, where she teaches women of the quiet and creative persuasion how to share the power of their personal story through speaking and visual storytelling. To learn more about her courses, workshops, or upcoming events or to book Wanda to speak, contact hello@mypowerplace.net and her website is www.WandaLovale.com

Believe in Love

REFLECTION

What did you learn about yourself from Wanda's chapter?

_____

_____

_____

Did you see yourself in Wanda's words?

_____

_____

_____

What are three things you will do to stay in action after what you learned from Wanda's chapter?

_____

_____

_____

_____

_____

_____

_____

_____

_____

Anesha Bonelli
Believe the Process of Forgiveness

I was about nine or 10 when the weight of my father's absence hit me full force. My elementary school at the time announced a father-daughter dance they were having. I can still remember the sting in my heart I felt as they were making the announcement. The rest of the kids in my class expressed how excited they were & couldn't wait to tell their dad about the upcoming event. I felt embarrassed and had to excuse myself to go into the restroom to allow my tears to flow freely without someone asking me what's wrong. That moment in the bathroom, I felt the loss of my father like I've never felt before. This was the first and last time I allowed myself to be hurt due to my father's absence. I can remember listening to Mariah Carey's song "Hero" and envision my father coming to save the day and fill the enormous void placed deep within my heart. I later spent several years hoping my father would miraculously appear and be a part of my life. I used to even pray that God would guide him back to me.

    I don't know the full story of why my mother and father split; I just remember when they did, I never saw him again. Initially, I never noticed the absence of a man I never really knew. I had a great upbringing; I lived in a loving home shared with my older sister. My mother worked two jobs to provide for us and was rarely home. However, when mom was home, we cooked and cleaned as a family. Mom created themed weekly dinner night's (ex. Sloppy-joe Saturday, seafood Sunday, etc.). During the summer months, mom would take my older sister and me, along with her sisters and a few cousins to Maryland. We would have cook-outs, race on auntie's scooters, and go to the pool around the corner from where we stayed. I was also a fierce reader, with my favorites being mystery and assassination genres.

But as the years went on, I again began to feel a gaping hole in my heart. I was at the beginning stages of puberty, and arguments between my mother and I ensued. In the pit of heated arguments between my mom and I, she would say I have my father's attitude. That statement would literally set my insides on fire. My response is, "how can I have the attitude of someone who is never around, nor calls, or even writes me. I believe this was when my pain turned into anger and resentment.

When I turned about 14-15 years old, my mother found out I am a lesbian and initially thought it was a faze. We argued so much I wound up moving in with my then-girlfriend at her mom's house. My girlfriend's mother didn't believe I was lesbian and, after staying with her for about 4-6 weeks, she scheduled me to meet a grown man I didn't know. When he came over to my girlfriend's house, her mother introduced us and told me I would be hanging out with him for a while. I never thought anything of it at the time and felt a little grown because I got to ride around in his car. We then leave, and he takes me to some bar he had to get on the highway to get to it. Once there, he then turns and asks me if I want something to drink; naturally, I said yes. At this time, I didn't know what a bar was or the effects of alcohol. The bartender never asked me for ID and made me a fruity drink, so I didn't taste the alcohol. I remember having about 2-3 of whatever that concoction was before we left and went back to his car. I can remember looking out of the window as I began to get dizzy and light-headed. As he drove on the highway, things were beginning to blur together. We stopped past my girlfriend's house, and I was so hungry at that time. I ran in quickly, ate 2 bowls of cereal, and went right back out to his car. As I was about to close my door, I had to open it back up because I was sick. I was unaware of the effects of alcohol and how it doesn't mix well with milk. But that was nothing in comparison to what happened next. Right after I finished throwing up, this stranger guy, my girlfriend's mother introduced me to, took me somewhere in Fairmount park. I don't know the exact part but know I was at a place that had a table with an awning covering the top. That's when it happened; I could feel him taking off my pants but was dizzy and out of it, I couldn't move.

I am trying to say no as my brain begins to comprehend what's going on. He then penetrates me. I let out a small scream as my hymen begins to break, and he continues to keep thrusting inside of me. I went from feeling pain to becoming numb and began to drift outside of my body. He finishes and immediately begins to dress himself as well as me. He takes me back to my girlfriend's house and drops me off, and I spent the entire night being sick. The next day after the alcohol wears off, and I noticed I am still sore in my private area, my girlfriend's mother called my girlfriend and me into her room. She then looks at my girlfriend and tells her, based on the conversation that the grown man and I had, that I was not a lesbian. Even while being accused, I remained silent about what happened to me. Thinking back on it now, I was taken advantage of in the worst way any child can be, and the only question that keeps repeating in my mind is, would this have happened if my father were a part of my life? Where were you when I needed you? Why didn't I have anybody to protect me from this predator? Was I not important enough? Was I not worth loving? Where were you?

The first time I saw my father since childhood was the year I turned twenty. My brother Kenyon from another mother searched and found both my mother and my father and his new family. Thanks to my brother connecting with our father, we were all set to visit our father on his birthday in August. I was completely stoked about seeing Kenyon since the last time I saw him, he was on his way to NYU for school. I wasn't thrilled about seeing my dad because of what happened to me and all the things he should have been there for and missed. My dad wasn't there when I was hospitalized, raped once and very close to a second, or when I simply graduated. I viewed him as a selfish man who had the choice to be in my life and chose not to be. I practiced for years what I would say to my father if I ever saw him again.

We arrive at my father's house, and I wait until I am sure everyone is comfortable, eating, and distracted before requesting that my father follow me outside so we could talk. In that moment, I released the pain that had been weighing on my heart due to his absence but didn't have the courage to tell my father about being raped. I did inform him how it felt to need him as a child and, at the young age of 20, felt he had missed out on the years he was needed, and at that point in my life, I didn't need him at all. You missed out on my greatest pain and most victorious triumphs. That day I bitterly watched how attentive he was to his youngest daughter. I even envied the attention he gave her, and that began to boil into anger. I initially didn't claim my youngest sister from another mother for the simple fact she got what I always wanted, dad's time. After that day I didn't contact him at all. We didn't speak again for another six to seven years when he was alerting us that he had lung cancer, and his therapy had taken a turn for the worst. My father was always a heavy beer drinker and cigarette smoker, which lead to his cancer. My youngest sister Alea had grown over the years and was now 15 years old. Due to the tragic news, my older sister Raynell recommended we begin to build a relationship with our youngest sister to ensure she knows she has a unit when our father is no longer here. So that's exactly what we did. We began calling and getting familiar with our little sister, and for the first time, she wanted to come to Philly and spend the night with us for her 16th birthday. We wanted to build a bond with our youngest, like the one my older sister and I had built over the years. Our first sister weekend together went off without a hitch. We had a weekend long slumber party with movies, sharing stories, and creating memories. My heart went out to Alea because the man she's always known as her father has been slowly dying right before her very eyes. The chemotherapy wasn't helping our dad, and by August of 2016, we were all faced with a tough decision. Our dad could no longer breathe on his own and was barely holding on. The doctors recommended we gather the family and have a meeting to discuss whether our father should live or die. My mother, two sisters, and our youngest sister's mom gathered in a room with the doctors on one side and us the family on the other. After telling us his current condition and the pros and cons of keeping him alive, they then went out of the room so we could make the final decision in private. We all collectively agreed the best thing to do would be to pull his plug and remove all the breathing tubes. The doctors asked us to go out of my father's room while they remove all the machines that were keeping our father alive.

Once they were finished, they allowed us to go back into our father's room. Alea climbed onto the hospital bed with our dad and cradled her head on his chest. I could tell the moment when our father breathed his last breath due to the heart-wrenching scream Alea let out as she sobbed into his arm. A dark cloud began to fill the room as my heart went out to my sisters and mother, who were in a pain that no number of tears could describe. It was in that instant I forgave my father for what he missed out on in my life and became grateful for the bonds formed amongst his 4 children. Although he had four kids by three different women, we, his kids, saw no difference, and the love we are blessed to share today is all possible due to our father. Thanks, dad, I love you, and more importantly, I forgive you.

Anesha is a dedicated Realtor who is responsible for aiding buyers, sellers, and investors in real estate transactions. She is on a mission to provide clients in the community the added benefits of becoming a homeowner/landlord. For Anesha, helping others is the most rewarding part of her role. She is focused on improving distressed neighborhoods and creating generational wealth.

Beyond that, she is a Philadelphia native, a daughter, proud aunt, wife, advocate for helping those in need, and proudly a part of

Melanated Mademoiselle (Alpha Omega Club). A non-profit geared towards educating African American girls ages 11-18 about their history, sisterhood, and entrepreneurship.

Please feel free to reach out to her via:

Email: anesha.bonelli@ymail.com

Facebook: Anesha Bonelli

LinkedIn: Anesha Bonelli

REFLECTION

What did you learn about yourself from Anesha's chapter?

_____

_____

_____

Did you see yourself in Anesha's words?

_____

_____

_____

What are three things you will do to stay in action after what you learned from Anesha's chapter?

_____

_____

_____

_____

_____

_____

_____

Camellia Burkett-Graham
Release the Bondage

I just remember being angry. No, let me change that. I was mad as hell! Months of early morning manna, hour of power, 4:30 am morning glory prayers down on my knees – all that! The ugly cries with snot running out my nose just begging God to help me keep my apartment and still not one word from Him! I was just tired, tired of struggling alone, tired of carrying the weight for others. Just t-i-r-e-d! Tired of struggling in this sea of thanklessness with no one to throw me a lifeline!

God *knew* I had been a good church member over the years. Yes, He *knew* that I paid tithes when I could, and yes, I was very involved in the church my father pastored for over 30+ years. I served long, hard, and strong. Multiple services on most Sundays; went out for weeknight fellowships; prayer meetings and bible study. I'm the one who usually picked up the van, picked up the people, and then parked the van long after the people were gone. You *know* that God! I can't cry anymore! I just can't! I'd been begging for His help and nothing! And He wanted *me* to be a minister? After all the hell those Negroes in that church have put my pastor/father and family through for long as I can remember, and now this! Huh! You know what, I'm done with praying, and I'm done with God!

I slammed shut the box I had been cramming stuff into and moved to the next one. Boxes were everywhere, stacked around the living room and in the hallway of the spacious apartment I occupied in Lefrak City, Queens. It was a fabulous 14th-floor corner apartment with its own balcony. I absolutely loved that apartment, and I loved me in it! Oh, well, so much for prayer changing things! It was in April 2013. A year I'd never forget!

I ended up relocating to Chesapeake, VA, with my second eldest and family. Bless her heart, she drove to New York in her pickup truck to get me and headed right back home. Don't get me wrong, I love my daughter and grands, but I wanted to be home; back in the only place I'd ever called home – smelly, dirty, crime-ridden New York! Little did I know then that relocating was the least of God's issues with me. I'd heard it said many times throughout my life that God will never force your will, but He definitely knows how to make you willing! I was about to find that out firsthand!

Admittedly, there were many advantages to being in VA. I was able to spend more than a telephone call worth of time with my two oldest granddaughters; I became part of a great church community under a dynamic pastor in Virginia Beach, and I gained a few loving daughters who still are very special to me. Yet, my spirit was unsettled.

But something just wasn't right! There was a weight-like pressure that had appeared on the back of my neck a few days after arriving in VA. I cannot tell you where it came from, honestly, but it was *very* unsettling. I had no idea what to do about it, but I knew something had to be done and soon! I didn't tell no one. As usual, I kept it to myself. Scrubbing the area didn't remove it, and exercising didn't sweat it away. I was getting really nervous. Naturally, when we are afraid, the first thing we do is reach for those familiar comforts of our roots, and knowing something about prayer, I immediately turned to God. Telling Him all about it after I repented, of course.

Within a short time following my repentance, the Spirit reminded me of another time I was under spiritual attack and experienced a type of pressure across my shoulders and up the back of my neck. It brought to light that I had been struggling with a stronghold back then too. What stronghold?" *I thought.* It was the stronghold of resistance.

See, I had failed to seriously understand in my ignorance that once I became sure of God's calling on my life years ago, I had a duty to respond immediately and not speak *against it*. Regardless of my reasons. And my resistance placed me in disobedience not only to the calling but also to God. For that alone, I deserved death. But instead of death, He gave me grace! Thank God for Jesus and the covenant of grace!

I called the young man who was now my pastor in VA and confessed. I said, "I believe I've been called to the ministry. I had to call you and tell you that." And *immediately,* the thing that had been sitting on the back of my neck lifted! It was amazing! I mean, there's no explanation for it other than my resistance! I had finally – after 10+ years – I finally *accepted* God's call to ministry.

Over time, the Holy Spirit continued working on me by helping me to see that my anger and hostility were not as a result of anything God had done; furthermore, I knew that! But would rather choke on it than admit it! Sad, right? You see, it was easier for me to blame God than face my own shortcomings.

What was even more mind-boggling was knowing what God knew about me from the inside out, and He still *chose me* for elevation! He knew I wasn't my circumstances. But I needed to know that! I wasn't that fabulous apartment in Lefrak, no more than I was the stuff I had crammed into those boxes. It was only through willfully releasing those *things* I'd been clinging to so tightly for years that I began to open up to the more tremendous potential and possibilities within me.

Release it because it will never let go of you!

Camellia Burkett-Graham is a native of Brooklyn, NY. Reading and writing has been a passion of hers since childhood.

This is Camellia's first publication as an author. Camellia believes that productive change is necessary and often comes at a price. We must embrace it.

As the mother of four and the grandmother of six, her desire is for them to believe that nothing is ever outside of their reach.

REFLECTION

What did you learn about yourself from Camellia's chapter?

_____

_____

_____

Did you see yourself in Camellia's words?

_____

_____

_____

What are three things you will do to stay in action after what you learned from Camellia's chapter?

_____

_____

_____

_____

_____

_____

_____

_____

Shanita Vital Davis
Embrace change

I had come to a place where I could no longer see the vision, at least the hope of the Vision. I was weary and exhausted. My life was like a parked car going nowhere. I had the weight of the world on my shoulders while still holding on to bad decisions created by underline insecurities. If I could compare my life to anything, it was like watching a toddler eat spaghetti. It was messy and all over the place with no control over anything. Life was so bad that I started experiencing heart palpitations and ended up in the ER for 3 days. I remember walking the hospital halls and there were glass windows where you could see the nurses monitoring patients. What I saw devastated me. I was informed that I was on the stroke and heart attack unit. I was 39 years old on a floor full of elderly people who may have lived most of their lives worrying about things that they couldn't change. This was the second time that this happened to me. I cried out for God's help. What I knew is that he would, but how, I did not know. I asked God for things before, and he gave them to me sometimes with ease, other times quite painfully, I did not get to choose. I just knew that I needed the help. For a year, God was shifting somethings in my life, and it did not feel good. There were so many highs and lows. I made a decision after leaving the hospital to shut down my daycare. To me, this was my moment of freedom. I had started a vision board and just followed what I thought was the plan. Things were going well. I was marketing daily for my Training service and had contracted myself to several daycares. Life was good then BOOM. This time it was catastrophic. I had almost lost it all, including my mind. I reopened my daycare in my home as a source of income. I was lost. I think to me I had come to what I would consider suicidal thoughts. I just remember telling God to put me to sleep! I remember losing my breath and feeling death. I asked God to let me live, and if he did, I would take care of my health, and I did. Having this near-death experience changed my life not all at once, but it was a start. Still fighting for significant change in my life, I had accumulated beautiful friendships from the most unlikely places, which was great. I didn't want to go through this journey alone; I wasn't selective; I just needed comfort. You see, God was holding a mirror up to my soul, and all I could see were broken pieces that I had held on tightly to for years that seemed to burst and mangle my palms from the tight grips of not letting go. I remember Mrs. Vaginia introducing me to a women's bible study book club, and they were reading the book "the Crushing by Bishop TD Jakes," and I felt as though I found purpose in the group. I wasn't an avid reader, but I could vent, and this was good enough for me. I honestly didn't care to read the book and had no plans on getting one. It's crazy how God knows his children because one of the members insisted that God told her to give me her book, and she said this with a grin that seemed to say, you're not getting over on anything. The book chapters seemed to be in sync with each obstacle of my journey its as if Mr. Jakes had written this book for me for this moment in time. I overcame so much through these ladies I made it my best to show up each week to the club to see my sisters. Things were beginning to shift for me. There was blockage though I was stagnant but didn't know why; I really can't explain, but I was somehow losing my vision. I remember cleaning out my garage one day. I had collected a few items to refurbish. One of the items I had kept from the time I moved in my home 8 years before I decided to throw some of the items away gave me the hardest time. I kept thinking, what if someone needs it or what if I can't find another one or what if I let it go and someone else gets it. I read Chapter 3 pg 45 that night, and it talked about how we must pay close attention to instability and an increase in the amount of mess placed upon us as it is a signal from the Lord that our growth might have stalled because of it.' The items in the garage were all I could think of, and why couldn't I let go. I found soon enough that the trauma from painful experiences showed up differently in many ways. It wasn't always volatile or passive. Sometimes it showed up in overcompensation and hoarding and just to fix the flaws that you were told that you had through the most unlikely sources such as discarded and broken furniture. The furniture was synonymous with people that I wanted to fix, especially the ones that hurt me. I was afraid that if I told them that I no longer needed them that they would somehow feel like I felt; unwanted and disregarded. So, the action of not letting go showed up on the inside of me, and it looked like strength to the outside world. I was suffocating myself and dying slowly mentally and spiritually from the hoard. So, this is where the heart palpitations, bad business deals, broken relationships, and abuse that I endured stemmed from. I no longer wanted this, so I dug deep and forgave the hurts. I had to come to the realization that those words that pierced my innocent soul came from broken people. I let go of those items in my garage first, and I felt a sense of relief. So funny how God uses the most unlikely experiences to catapult you in the direction of healing. I then made a list of all that needed to be forgiven and released unwanted people, places, and things. I had one last release, the forgiveness of me. I owed it to myself to be ok with letting go. I was free; I could see clearer. I could find so many treasures laid up for me that were covered by the gripping pains of trauma that caused so much fear and insecurities. I encourage you, the reader, to look so deep within you and find the thing that irritates you, clouds your vision, that thing that hurts the most, and LET IT GO and make room for the vision I encourage to RELEASE!

Shanita Vital Davis (The Classroom Management Diva),

Shanita is a native of Houston TX. Historic Third Ward, and Early Childhood Education training and coaching is her passion. This is her first publication as an author. As a wife, mother of a blended family of 5 and the grandmother of 4, her desire is to show the reader that PAIN HAS PURPOSE and that each overcoming experience is designed for those connected to your purpose!

REFLECTION

What did you learn about yourself from Shanita's chapter?

_____

_____

_____

Did you see yourself in Shanita's words?

_____

_____

_____

What are three things you will do to stay in action after what you learned from Shanita's chapter?

_____

_____

_____

_____

_____

_____

_____

_____

Dr. Victoria Sherlock
Accept What God Allows
Your story does not belong to you

"The girl who rarely smiled." As the youngest of five children, my parents already had high expectations for me. I have two brothers and two sisters. I was born in South Philadelphia and raised in Southwest and North Philadelphia.

While living in Southwest, I endured sexual abuse and rape from a couple of my neighbors. A part of me thought it was normal, and I honestly didn't see anything wrong with it because it went on for so long. I was told that I was sexy and I was "getting got" before I got older and "got got" as well that if I told, there was going to be harm done to one of my family members that I was really close with. As I grew up and learned that what was done to me was not my fault and it was wrong, I started to hate the word sexy because every time I heard it, I would think of the situations I was in. My mother always embedded in me how important education is, so I always liked school (she worked at each school I went to up until the sixth grade!). While in elementary school, I witnessed my mother fighting with a man, and I never thought he would fight my mom. I then started to believe that it was normal for a man to put his hands on a female. I later learned that men fighting women was not normal.

I am now in my first year of college at Geneva College near Pittsburgh, Pa. While playing basketball, I began having terrible stomach pains, so I went to the nurse. She did a blood test and came back and said, "Ms. Sherlock did you know you are pregnant?" I told her no at least five times because I was in denial. I left the nurse's office and went to the Walgreens to take two more tests. I guess it was safe to say that I was really pregnant and could not deny it any longer. My first semester in college, and here I was, leaving in May six months pregnant. When I came back home to Philly, my brother let me stay with him because my mom was so disappointed in me, she told me I could not come back. Two weeks later, she called me and told me to come home. I had my daughter in August and knew I wanted to continue my education, but I did not have a path. My daughter's father and I began to have a toxic relationship, and I started getting physically abused. I still had self-esteem issues, so I thought I was doing something wrong and needed to fix myself and that I was the problem. At the Earn center was where I found out about the CDA course. I enrolled in the CDA course. Towards the end of the course, Harcum College came in and spoke about the programs that they had to offer. I then enrolled in Harcum College and earned my Associates degree in Early Childhood Education. After Harcum college, I attended St. Joseph's University. But the closer I came towards graduation, the more time it would have taken me to be on campus, and I could not do that with working a full-time job and taking care of my daughter, so I unenrolled. While working at Brightside Academy, Grand Canyon University came to talk about their program. So two months later, I attended Grand Canyon University. I earned my Bachelor's degree from Grand Canyon in Elementary Education and Special Education. I stayed to earn my Masters' degree in Gifted Education. I will be done in November of 2020 at Gwynedd Mercy University and earn my Doctoral degree in Educational Leadership in PK-12 school systems.

I attended a book signing with the author Tiona Brown for her book, "Please don't touch me there." I have heard peoples' stories, and one lady was explaining to the audience that her coping mechanism from her abuse, as well as other things that she had to endure beginning from a young age, was never smiling and staying to herself. When she said that, a light bulb went off in my head that said, "Oh my God, is this the reason why I rarely smile"? I think it was. For as long as I can remember, people have been telling me to smile and "it wasn't that bad." Basketball, crying, keeping quiet, and eating were my coping mechanisms to deal with my pain. I moved to Delaware and began developing a church family that taught me how to have a relationship with God. That was very challenging to do for me because I always asked myself, "why do bad things always happen to good people?" God has placed Obioma Martin, Bishop Blake Mills, Lady Carolyn Mills, my therapist, etc. in my life that could help me unpack my trauma and to grow and mature. I lost my mother in April of 2020. She was my cheerleader and motivation for me to continue to move forward to earn my doctorate degree. Over the past thirty years, I have endured pain, hurt, abuse (mental, emotional, physical, and spiritual), been in bondage, betrayal, depression, suicide attempts, happiness, love, health issues that shall remain unidentified, peer pressure, etc. I have come to learn that all my experiences and everything that has happened in my life are not for me. I am a living testimony, and every day, I strive to be a better steward, mother, friend, daughter, sister, aunt, educator, supporter, etc. I am a walking miracle, and I am on this Earth to teach and help others. Something that I plan to do until it is my time to be with the Lord. This is a part of my story, one I am no longer ashamed of nor afraid to share. I love you. Smile and laugh in the face of adversity. You are destined for greatness and fearfully and wonderfully made. Stay blessed.

Victoria Sherlock is a Philly native, now residing in Delaware. She is a single mother and youth ministry leader at her church, Tree of Life Ministries. Ms. Sherlock earned her Doctorate degree in educational leadership from Gwynedd Mercy University. She plans to continue to help, mentor, teach, coach, and guide the youth to live to the best of their abilities and strive to be great and make a difference in the world.

REFLECTION

What did you learn about yourself from Victoria's chapter?

_____

_____

_____

Did you see yourself in Victoria's words?

_____

_____

_____

What are three things you will do to stay in action after what you learned from Victoria's chapter?

_____

_____

_____

_____

_____

_____

_____

_____

La Vonne A. Weaver
Take Action
Turning Challenges Into Works of Art

"Sticks and stones may break my bones, but words will never hurt me." Growing up, this was my mantra whenever a classmate said something unkind to me.

Reflecting upon this statement, I would have rather had the sticks and stones. Unfortunately, my childhood mantra was incorrect; words do hurt. Words are very powerful and can profoundly impact our mental, emotional, and spiritual well-being. Careless words are like thieves; they can rob us of our peace, joy, and creativity.

Several years ago, I found myself repeating my childhood mantra when my six-year relationship came to an unexpected end. Someone I had been dating at the time had found a new interest and decided to make it public on Valentine's Day. My only notification was a photo on social media. I approached him with the hopes of engaging in some healthy dialogue about the picture, and he surprised me. My former friend had already prepared his defense, which consisted of berating me and *reminding me why I was fortunate to have had someone like him*. Even when we spoke at later times, he went to great lengths to justify his actions by stating that he had finally met someone who could *"light up a room."*

It is amazing how one experience can crack open so many wounds that I thought healed. This incident took me back to my childhood when I was ridiculed for my too-small clothes, or I was always the last one to get chosen for a team. Initially, I thought it would have been easier if my former friend had just left the relationship. Then, it would have spared me the pain, insults, heartache, manipulation, the financial mess, and embarrassment. I spent countless days analyzing what I did wrong. I picked myself apart by replaying the images that I saw on Valentine's Day, and I compared myself to his new love interest. Eventually, this had taken its toll on me; I lost my appetite; my energy was low, and I dropped about 40 pounds. Unbeknownst to me, I had also developed an irregular heartbeat that would require a cardiologist.

I indeed would have chosen a different experience, but God transformed a challenge into a work of art through my passion for creating.

Canvas 1: *Exhale and Evaluate Where You Are*

"The only thing that is constant is change." Change is a natural part of life. No matter how prepared we might be, unexpected shifts will happen. I had to accept the reality that my relationship had come to an end; Facebook had served me a time-out notice. With one photo, my life had changed.

We have to be careful not to allow sudden shifts and disappointments to make us bitter. Although I did not foresee this unexpected change, I realized that there was little I could do to stop it. Many thoughts ran through my mind, from how to reconcile the mess to how to *return the "favor."* I had a see-saw of emotions for months. Being still and breathing were indeed my best options at the time, trust me.

I permitted myself to feel without judgment. Gradually I started to accept each day as it came; this did not happen overnight. Step by step, each day was better. Allow yourself to feel without judgment. Breathe in life, peace, and joy. Exhale anything that is causing you pain.

Canvas 2: Do Your Own Investigation of the Truth

*"**The Power of life and death are in the tongue.**"* The reality that my life had changed in the blink of an eye was challenging. I continued to struggle with the justifications that my former friend shared, and I wanted a truthful explanation. I could not understand why it took him six years to discover that I was *"unattractive, worthless, and did not light up a room...."* Yet, I let those words seep into my mind and impact my health.

When I was able to still my mind, I began to challenge the words that he spoke to me. I held his words up against GOD's word. For every unkind statement that my former friend spoke, I consulted God's word. In several conversations, my former friend told me, **"I was unattractive, but I tried hard to put myself together with the best that I could."** However, the word of God said, "**I am fearfully and wonderfully made.**" Another passage referred to me as God's "**Masterpiece.**"

Even though I was not surprised that his words did not align with God's words, I still allowed myself to fall prey to them. We have to be careful about what version of the truth we accept about ourselves.

God guided me to use my passion for art and writing as an outlet. This became a safe space and a source of healing. I journaled my thoughts daily. I created collages, word clouds, inspirational infographics, and posted them everywhere to remind me of who *I was* according to the word of God.

What messages do you believe about yourself? Are those beliefs aligned with what God says and thinks about you?

Canvas 3: *Channel Your Energy Into Something Positive.*

"***What you focus on grows****."* Starting over was not easy. I was approaching 50 and found myself suddenly single again. Instead of asking God, why me? I chose to ask; how could I meet this challenge with grace and move forward?

What was intended for harm, God used it to reignite a fire within me. While I was in the relationship, I put my creativity and dreams on the backburner. I rarely spent quiet time with God. The relationship was my priority.

After we separated, I experienced periods of depression and sadness, but I also allowed myself space to create each day. The unkind words became my fuel. I sat in front of a mirror, and I began to write messages on strips of paper that affirmed who I was. I took every unkind statement my former friend threw at me, and I rewrote it as a positive affirmation, beginning with the words ***I AM***. I was determined not to allow someone else's behavior to finish my chapter. Transforming the statements began to neutralize the power they had over me. Yes, my inner critic would often try to visit me and repeat what my former friend spoke to me. Moment by moment, I learned to speak to my higher self.

Are there chapters of your life that you need to close?

Canvas 4: Be Open to a New Way of Being.

"Behold, I do a new thing." Creativity has always soothed my soul. I have been creating since I was about five. Even in the darkest moments of this mess, creating lifted my spirits. Creativity was a gentle reminder that God was at work on my behalf. Every day, when I came home from work, I was excited about creating something new, even though I did not know what it would make. During this time, I communed with God. I asked questions, I cried, prayed, listened, and I followed instructions.

Spending time in my creative space with God took my focus off the challenges and allowed room for productive thoughts to flow. I did not immediately recognize that my difficulties were being transformed into works of art. This process of crying and creating went on for months before I realized that God was preparing me to be of service to others.

God would not allow me to waste this heartbreak and the experience. If it had been up to me, I would have chosen to repair the relationship. As God listened to my concerns and prayers, he was crafting a whole creative plan that would call me to inspire others called Liv Vibrantly. I was upset, and God was redirecting everything. I began creating greeting cards, shirts, cards, keepsake affirmation boxes, and prayer tiles.

This experience pushed me out of my comfort zone and tested every fiber of my faith. Not only did I rediscover my passion for creating, but I reconnected with God. I learned to love myself again and get to know who God created me to be. I no longer needed to be validated by others. I now understood that my light always shines and lights up every room that I enter. Most of all, it changed my perspective on how I viewed challenges. I now see challenges as opportunities to create something beautiful to share with the world.

Is there something that you are passionate about?

What challenge can you turn into a masterpiece?

Canvas 5: Be the Solution to Someone's Problem.

Perhaps you are facing some challenges or have been discouraged by some unkind words or actions? When you make it through, you become the solution for someone else. This journey reminded me that I was not alone. I surrounded myself with a loving and supportive community. One of the best ways to counteract negatively is to transform it into something beautiful. You will be amazed at how many people are watching you and cheering for you.

You do not have to be an artist by trade to create. Anything that you do well is your artistry and your platform. Whether it is baking, teachings, customer service, do it with excellence! Wherever you go, you will make a splash; the question is, will you be a good representative when you show up? Do not allow painful experiences to taint your beauty. There is someone who needs you to be a splash of paint on their canvas. Why not you?

La Vonne A. Weaver is the Chief Encouragement Officer and Creative Energy behind Liv Vibrantly. She creates for change! Born and raised in St. Louis, Missouri. La Vonne is an educator, writer, and artist. She has over 25 years of experience in education plus 15 years in retail and customer service. Her mission is to empower, encourage, and elevate everyone she meets. La Vonne loves to use her passion for art and words to make a meaningful difference each day.

REFLECTION

What did you learn about yourself from La Vonne's chapter?

_____
_____
_____

Did you see yourself in La Vonne's words?

_____
_____
_____

What are three things you will do to stay in action after what you learned from La Vonne's chapter?

_____
_____
_____
_____
_____
_____
_____

"LORD my God, I called to you for help, and you healed me."
— Psalm 30:2

Mavis A. Creagh
Heal from Self Pain

What do you do when anguish and disappointment is caused by your own hands? When there is nobody to blame, no fingers to point, and nobody responsible but yourself? Self-Evaluation and Reflection has helped me to heal and become my best self. Many things that were sent to break me came from external sources (Rape, Sexual Assault, Severe Abuse). However, what about gluttony, self-hatred, the idolatry of men, alcoholism, disobedience, or promiscuity? All these may stem from past hurts but are ultimately a result of my own decisions and choices. Whatever the situation, let the Most High shine so bright even within the worst situations to heal, restore, and renew. The Creator is not mocked and will see you through even the worst valleys. Heartache, pain, desperation, and loneliness will lead you to some of the lowest valleys, but there is a "Balm in Gilead!" Love yourself, and always remember God loves you in **All Situations** and will never leave you nor forsake you!

Healing Through Hurt

Healing is an ongoing process.

1. Take time to regroup and regain your focus. Have you ever seen a chicken with its head cut off.. Yeah, that is how I look sometimes!

2. Focus on what brings you joy. If you feel hopeless and devastated, try to find one thing you are thankful for that makes you happy.

3. Think about how you can have peace.

Here are some questions that have helped me along my journey.

1. Do you need to remove yourself from situations?
2. Are there relationships that will cause more confusion in your life?
3. How can you separate from negative triggers?
4. What specific practices will allow you to be more centered and focused?

With all of this, take time to assess your current situation in life.

1. If you are hurting, acknowledge it. Do you need to seek therapy, counseling, or professional help?
2. Do you need to reprioritize your duties? Are you doing everything else for people and not prioritizing yourself?
3. Are you handling the hurt or ignoring it altogether? Some things cannot simply be pushed under the rug.
4. What realities of life have you been avoiding that can help you in your healing process?
   - One sign of ignoring your reality is constant busyness to the point of exhaustion. This is a method that some people use to hide hurt and stifle their healing journey. I personally, at one point, was always busy to the point where I did not have time to think about anything else, especially dealing with hurtful people, pain, and experiences.

Move Forward Through Your Pain

1. Take time and **BREATHE** IN THE MOMENT!!!

2. You cannot outwork your pain!

3. Take your time and just BE!!! **Be** who you are, **Be** present in your feelings, **Be** who the Creator has made you to be. Just BE....

4. Be Patient with Yourself. Healing is a Process, not a microwave fix. If you try and skip steps, feelings, and emotions, the likelihood of not reaching your goal of true healing is decreased. Some feelings and emotions I never want to experience again. But allowing them to surface during my healing journey has allowed me to better accept my past and move forward into a more peaceful, whole, and happy Future!

Walk Daily In Grace

1. Give yourself a Break!!! Nobody is perfect.

2. Stop beating yourself up. This is not the work of the Most High! Your Creator wants to see you whole and at peace. Walk Daily with the full grace and mercy of the Father in Heaven.

3. Treat yourself with the same kindness as you treat others.

4. Rest in the Arms of the Most High!

Whatever you do along your healing journey, remember to stay focused on loving yourself. There may be times of doubt and uncertainty, but God is not a God that he shall lie. His promises are Yes and Amen! He will not withhold any good thing, and he wants you Healed!

Do not relinquish your joy to serve others. Be at peace with allowing yourself to heal and walk boldly in the direction of your divine purpose.

> "God is our refuge and strength,
> an ever-present help in trouble" ... Psalm 46:1-3

Weak in My Sleep- God is a Restorer

Sometimes the season where we stand still is the time when the Most High can do the most in our Life! "Let Not Your Heart Be Troubled." Remember this when you are spiritually asleep and awaiting a great breakthrough. Remain faithful to the WORD and cling to the Creator. Remember who you are and whose you are. Rely on the Father and Remember the Precepts that have been instructed unto you. **Love Yourself and Live Your Best Life!!!**

Lean on the Spirit of the Holy Ghost and shift to the Divine Purpose manifested unto you. In time of emotional and mental sleep...**REST**. Do not think that the Father is not working. Hold Steadfast to the Instruction and Word of the Most High.

Love Yourself through whatever situation or circumstance that has been endured. If you have made it out alive and in your right mind, then you are yet blessed. Many people who went through the same situations as I experienced did not make it. I am a survivor of sexual and domestic violence. I have endured unexplainable evils, and yet here I stand with peace and joy. Do I still experience remnants from my hurt and pain? Of course, there is no magic eraser or wand to remove the memories and emotional scars. However, I decided that I would not allow these experiences to kill me or debilitate me.

Some people are walking, moving, breathing but are dead inside. Some people have zoned out for so long that they have become numb to constant attacks on their spirit and body. Wherever you are in life, do not give up and do not give in. If you are still in a situation that is hurtful and destructive, please take the necessary steps to leave and take care of yourself. There are multiple resources locally and nationally to support your recovery. Do not ever feel like you deserve mistreatment or must settle to be included even in work, family, or friendship relations. You deserve to be whole, to be happy, and to be healed. If you have experienced extreme hurt from others or yourself, the first step is to forgive yourself and stop pretending that the hurt was not real. This will only further push back your recovery and keep you further bound. I remember almost two years ago when I was coming out of a horrible situation, I fought for my life, my mind, and my health. I was not going down without a fight! Fast forward to today… I am stronger than ever and thankful that I fought for myself and for others who had been hurt and needed to know how to heal.

Mavis A. Creagh is an advocate, survivor, inspirational leader, motivational speaker, mentor, entrepreneur, consultant, and 2X bestselling author! She currently serves as the Executive Director of R3SM, Inc. (Recover, Rebuild, Restore Southeast MS) in Hattiesburg, MS.

She is the Founder & CEO of We Women Ministries LLC, a ministry created to empower, enrich, and elevate women from all backgrounds.

She is the proud mother of a teenage son, Jordan, and they reside in Hattiesburg, MS.

Contact Information

Facebook: Mavis Creagh

LinkedIn: Mavis Creagh

Instagram: mavisaloves

Email:maviscreaghmedia@gmail.com

REFLECTION

What did you learn about yourself from Mavis's chapter?

_____

_____

_____

Did you see yourself in Mavis's words?

_____

_____

_____

What are three things you will do to stay in action after what you learned from Mavis's chapter?

_____

_____

_____

_____

_____

_____

_____

_____

Pastor Cynthia D. Allen
Elevation requires Alleviation

My story begins with me really at the beginning of what I call my life change when I had done what I felt everybody else wanted me to do. You know, I had been the Good Wife, I've been a mom, and I stood by my husband. I was a great supportive daughter. I was good in church work, but I had come to a place where I necessarily was not happy. Then in the midst of all my unhappiness, real life began to happen. You know, the kids were grown up. Everybody had made their changes, and everything around me was changing, not necessarily elevating but changing, but I wasn't changing. While I was on my way to change, my son Andrew got shot. He got shot five times by his cousin, which was my first cousin's son. It was at that moment, I was in a place where before I could think about myself or worry about where I was, I had to again pause in my own elevation to now take care of my 20-something-year-old son. I'm in the middle of what I call a family turmoil or family war because this is my cousin's son, who was his best friend, who they got into it over a girl, and literally, my son almost died.

I remember that night, the morning we got the call, it was about three or four o'clock in the morning, and my daughter was in her room. She was in her room, and she came in screaming. And I'll never forget the scream. She started screaming, and she said, Mom, Drew's been shot. And for me, all I heard was Drew got shot and killed. And so we get the call middle of the night, we started heading to the hospital. From the call, they took drew to Einstein hospital. When I got there, I had this traumatic experience with him. Then they said right then and there, he passed out. They said he literally was about to die, and they rushed him into surgery.

The next 12 months were filled with physical therapy and physically washing and feeding him. We had to take care of this

23-year-old man like he was a six-month-old baby. Though he was a grown man, this was a lot. It became overwhelming and taxing on our entire family emotionally, physically, and spiritually. I knew that I had not really let go. I felt like I was in a world war with my husband's family, who became aggravated and agitated by what had happened with my son on their side, and they wanted some kind of revenge against my cousins, my mother's side of the family. I remember my mother coming in and saying, we're not dealing with this; we're not dealing with that. You get a moment to cry. And then we've got to put this child back together again. And so that was the first step that I made towards my elevation journey. I made a decision that I was not going to engage in the foolishness, but that I had to choose to elevate myself above the wrong that had been done. I wasn't going to allow this devasting event to divide my cousin and I. My cousin and I were innocent bystanders. We had nothing to do with the relationship that went left between our sons, and we had not done anything to each other. Our sons created this crisis. Moreover, my cousin and I were best friends, and I did not want to lose our relationship over foolishness.

I remember my mom helping to make the choice to elevate. My mom talked me out of being in the middle of the crisis. My mom said our focus needs to be getting Drew healthy again. My mom said we will stand on the word and pray for him and us to get through this.

Then I was referred to Dr. Tonya Ladipo for family counseling and therapy. I absolutely love her. My son and I went for therapy, and you know black people don't really get therapy. We don't do that in our families, but we had a therapy session. We both were sitting on the couch. And it was at that moment that she told me that I had not left that moment, I had not breathed, and I had not gone on. I could have at that moment rejected her. I could have at that moment shut down and totally rejected her. I honestly didn't know what she was talking about. But I chose to hear what she was saying and go with it.

I knew I had to do something different because I was literally on a treadmill. I was going nowhere fast. And in order for me to really go forward, I had to elevate by getting help. Seeing a therapist helped me to release the pain and the stress from my belly and my soul. Therapy was the catalyst for change for me. Tonya invited Drew and I to participate in an exercise that would help us to process the trauma. Tonya instructed Drew and I to hold hands, and she said, you know, let's go back to that moment. And when she looked at my face, she said, I can see that you have not taken a moment in six months to just breathe. And I had literally told this story before that I had literally not realized that I have just been shallowly panting. Still, I had to learn how to breathe again.

I could not start my elevation journey without first pausing to breathe. As we sat there and I tell Tonya the story on the couch, she instructed us to take deep breaths. I remember waking up, crying soaking wet, looked like time had passed, and I had to literally let that moment go. I could have chosen to stay there. I could have chosen not to forgive my cousin, son. I could have chosen to be bitter against that side of the family. But I chose to elevate by alleviating the frustration, anxiety, anger, fear, and animosity. I had to alleviate all those things because holding on to it was holding me down like a weight at the bottom of the sea. It was time for me to literally elevate to where God really wanted to take me. And then in my elevation, I saw that, as I began to go up, God had so much more. And really wanted to use me as a catalyst for change.

Elevation requires alleviation. We have to alleviate all the stinking thinking to elevate from the sting of any situation. You have to alleviate all that you've gone through, and you have to alleviate the pain of what you've gone through. Yes, you've gone through it, yes it happened, you won't forget it. Philippians 3:13 tells us to forget those things which are behind and to reach forth unto those things which are ahead.

Pastor Cynthia D. Allen is a 4th generation woman of God who is devoted to the vision of Kingdom building. She is the founder and CEO of two corporations. C.A.N. (Cynthia Allen Network) Cynthia Allen Success Academy Childcare Center. She's also Co-Owner of "Precious Food Service," where her husband provides meals to over 10,000 seniors a month. She is the Co-Pastor with her husband, Pastor Willis E. Allen, Sr. of Victory Through Faith Church.

REFLECTION

What did you learn about yourself from Cynthia's chapter?

_____

_____

_____

Did you see yourself in Cynthia's words?

_____

_____

_____

What are three things you will do to stay in action after what you learned from Cynthia's chapter?

_____

_____

_____

_____

_____

_____

_____

_____

Are you ready to believe in you again? Are you ready to break free from relationships that choke you up and hold you back? Are you ready to learn how to accept all that God has for you and move into a new season of action, healing, and elevation? Are you ready to B.R.E.A.T.H.E?

Unlock the powerful principles of the B.R.E.A.T.H.E journey toward self-discovery and set yourself free from stress, bondage, and the unnecessary and uncomfortable issues life throws your way. You don't have to stay stuck, and you don't have to live your life in hiding.

This is your season of breakthrough and renewal, but first, you have to learn how to B.R.E.A.T.H.E.

I'm so excited to take this journey along with you and help you to believe in yourself, release toxic things and people from your life, accept the past and move forward, take action and stay in control, heal old wounds, and ultimately, elevate to abundance and a rejuvenated life. Are you ready to see significant changes in your life? Are you ready to B.R.E.A.T.H.E in new ambition and live the prosperous life promised by God?

The time is now. Change requires action, so let' start together. Register for either one of my online courses, group coaching, or maybe you are ready to tell your own story. Either way, I would love to support you on your journey to becoming the best version of yourself.

Get started today! http://bit.ly/GroupCoachingWithObioma

More products by Dr. Obioma Martin

- I.M.E. Journal

Implementation, Manifestation, and Elevation are the three keys to having everything your heart desires. Do you have a vision, dreams, and goals that have not manifested? Have you ever felt stuck or just existing? Have you ever felt like your life was programmed like a robot or computer? This journal is just what you need to get unstuck, motivated, energized, and pressing forward until all of your goals and dreams are realized.

- B.R.E.A.T.H.E book

B.R.E.A.T.H.E. is such an easy read that you could literally read it in a day. However, reading it in a day will be a disservice as the book is written to take you on a journey of healing. Healing for you as well as anyone in your circle of influence. Each chapter summarizes a B.R.E.A.T.H.E. principle brought to life by Obioma's life story and provides practical application, prayer, and scripture references for the reader.

- B.R.E.A.T.H.E Journal

This 28-day wellness journal is a self-guided journal that helps you focus your thoughts and time on prayer and meditation.

- 5 P's of Prosperity Journal

This journal helps you learn how to pause so you can be still and process your thoughts, you will be guided in prayer and planning so you can position yourself to prosper.

- Prosperity 90-day Planner

This planner provides clarity, focus, and accountability

- 30-Day Elevation Challenge

This challenge helps you to rediscover, explore, and reinvent yourself personally, professionally, and spiritually.

Contact Obioma Martin at obioma@obiomamartin.com

Follow her on FB@obiomamartin,

IG@iamobiomamartin

Website www.omazingyou.com

www.ingramcontent.com/pod-product-compliance
Lightning Source LLC
Chambersburg PA
CBHW042327150426
43193CB00001B/12